The Princes in the Tower:
An Unsolved Mystery

Contents

Written by Abbie Rushton

Illustrated by Giorgio Bacchin

Collins

1 Meet the narrator – Elizabeth Woodville

Hello. I am Elizabeth Woodville. I live in **Tudor** England.

The year is 1487 and Henry VII is on the throne. But before he became king, two groups had been fighting about who would be king.

I am the mother of Edward V, who was meant to be king. But my son never became king. He and my other son, Richard of Shrewsbury, disappeared. They were last seen in 1483. Please can you help me find out who was responsible for their disappearance?

I will tell you about some of the key **suspects**.

FACT!
These are called "Roman numerals" because the Romans used them. Now we use them to show the difference between kings and queens with the same name:

I = 1st	**VI** = 6th
II = 2nd	**VII** = 7th
III = 3rd	**VIII** = 8th
IV = 4th	**IX** = 9th
V = 5th	**X** = 10th

All the suspects are **descended** from King
Edward III. That's what caused all the fighting.
Lots of people thought *they* should be king.

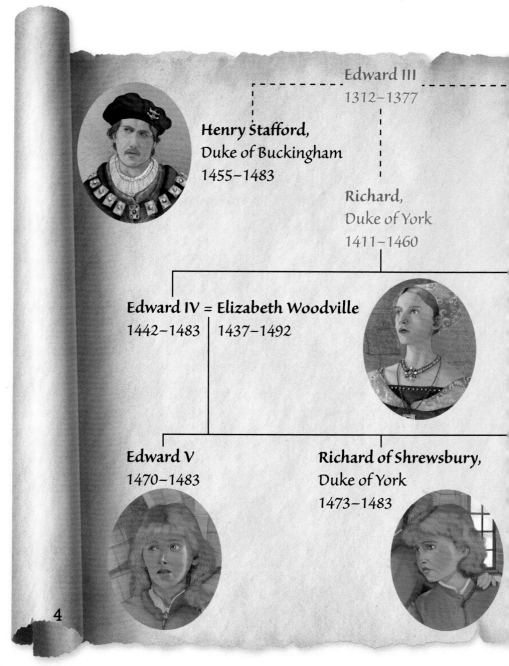

Edward III
1312–1377

Henry Stafford,
Duke of Buckingham
1455–1483

Richard,
Duke of York
1411–1460

Edward IV = Elizabeth Woodville
1442–1483 | 1437–1492

Edward V
1470–1483

Richard of Shrewsbury,
Duke of York
1473–1483

This is a family tree. It shows who married who and what children they had. The = sign means that two people married. The dates show when they were born and when they died. The dotted lines show that these people weren't direct descendants.

Margaret Beaufort = **Edmund Tudor**
1443–1509   1431–1456

Richard III
1452–1485

Elizabeth of York = **Henry VII**
1466–1503   1457–1509

So, the key suspects are:

- Richard III – my husband's brother
- Margaret Beaufort and her son, Henry VII
- Henry Stafford, Duke of Buckingham.

All were hungry for power. All were related to King Edward III. All of them had a **motive** for making my boys disappear.

Richard III

Henry Stafford, Duke of Buckingham

Margaret Beaufort & Henry VII

Timeline

9th April 1483:
Edward IV dies

I will tell you what happened. On 9th April 1483, my husband, King Edward IV, died. My eldest son, Edward V, was going to be the next king. He travelled to the Tower of London to prepare to be **crowned** king.

FACT!
The Tower of London is a large castle in London. It was a palace for the royal family to live in, but it was also a prison.

the Tower of London

Because my son Edward was only 12 years old, my husband's brother, Richard, would rule for Edward until he was old enough. But Richard betrayed us and locked Edward away in the Tower.

Fearful for our lives, I fled with my other children, to hide in Westminster Abbey.

Elizabeth Woodville seeks safety at Westminster Abbey.

Timeline

9th April 1483:	30th April 1483:	1st May 1483:	16th June 1483:	22nd June 1483:	6th July 1483:
Edward IV dies	Richard takes Edward V to the Tower	Elizabeth takes her children to Westminster Abbey	Richard, Duke of York, joined Edward at the Tower of London	The princes' claim to the throne in doubt	Richard is crowned king

8

I was asked to let my younger son, Richard of Shrewsbury, join his brother in the Tower. I did not want to let him go, but in June I finally agreed.

Later that month, people were told that my marriage to Edward IV was **illegal**. This meant that neither of my sons had a true claim to the throne.

A few weeks later, Richard III was crowned king.

a replica of Richard III's crown

Timeline

9th April 1483:	30th April 1483:	1st May 1483:	16th June 1483:	22nd June 1483:	6th July 1483:
Edward IV dies	Richard takes Edward V to the Tower	Elizabeth takes her children to Westminster Abbey	Richard, Duke of York, joined Edward at the Tower of London	The princes' claim to the throne in doubt	Richard is crowned king

In July 1483, there was an attempt to rescue the princes from the Tower. The plan was to set fires around the Tower and free the princes in the chaos.

Historians don't know much about the plan, apart from the fact that it failed. They don't even know whose plan it was.

July 1483:
Rescue attempt!

My sons were last seen practising **archery** in the garden of the Tower of London in July 1483. After that, they simply disappeared.

I will not make any **accusations** about who I think was responsible – I value my life too much. I will explain the evidence against my three main suspects, then you can make up your own minds.

Timeline

9th April 1483:	30th April 1483:	1st May 1483:	16th June 1483:	22nd June 1483:	6th July 1483:
Edward IV dies	Richard takes Edward V to the Tower	Elizabeth takes her children to Westminster Abbey	Richard, Duke of York, joined Edward at the Tower of London	The princes' claim to the throne in doubt	Richard is crowned king

July 1483:
Rescue attempt!

Mid-July 1483:
Last sighting
of the princes

13

2 Suspect 1: Richard III

Background

Richard was very loyal to my husband, Edward IV. When Edward lost his throne, Richard helped him to get it back again.

Richard was a good soldier, even though he had some problems with his spine. He was a very good leader as he had been successful in ruling the north of England.

Claim to the throne: strong

Richard was the king's brother. If the king's two sons were not there to claim the throne, Richard would become king. Plus, the king had already named Richard as the person who should rule the country until my son was old enough.

Richard III

15

Evidence

Richard could not be trusted. When he met my son, Edward V, on his way to the Tower of London, Richard said he would make sure his nephew arrived safely. Instead, he locked Edward up in the Tower.

Richard was definitely not our favourite uncle!

Richard claimed he was keeping Edward safe in the Tower. This was normal for kings before they were crowned, but Richard kept delaying the ceremony. I do not think he ever intended to allow Edward to become king.

Richard's defence

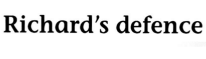

Hello. My name is Richard III. I would like to defend myself against these accusations. I think Elizabeth Woodville and her family wanted to control Edward V after he became king. This was not what my brother, the last king, wanted, so I protected Edward.

Also, a few weeks after Edward V came to the Tower, Elizabeth allowed her other son, Richard of Shrewsbury, to join him. Is this really the action of a mother who was worried for the safety of her children?

3 Suspect 2: Henry VII and Margaret Beaufort

Background

Margaret Beaufort's husband died just months before she gave birth to Henry VII. he was absolutely determined that her son would become king.

Margaret Beaufort

Claim to the throne: weak

Henry was distantly related to Edward III through the women in his family. It was not a strong link. Henry's father may have been born outside of marriage, which made Henry's claim even weaker.

Henry VII

Rebellion

I was good friends with Margaret Beaufort. Soon after Richard III took the crown, we made a plan that our children, Elizabeth of York and Henry Tudor (who would become Henry VII), would marry. It would make Henry's claim to the throne much stronger.

In October 1483, there was still no sign of my boys. Margaret and I joined a rebellion called Buckingham's Rebellion. We wanted to remove Richard III from the throne and make Henry Tudor king instead. If my son could not be a king, I wanted to make sure my daughter would be a queen.

We planned to attack from France, but a storm stopped the **uprising**.

Timeline

9th April 1483:	30th April 1483:	1st May 1483:	16th June 1483:	22nd June 1483:	6th July 1483:
Edward IV dies	Richard takes Edward V to the Tower	Elizabeth takes her children to Westminster Abbey	Richard, Duke of York, joined Edward at the Tower of London	The princes' claim to the throne in doubt	Richard is crowned king

A storm stopped a planned attack from France.

July 1483:
Rescue attempt!

Mid-July 1483:
Last sighting
of the princes

18th October 1483:
Attempted Buckingham's
Rebellion

Evidence: Margaret Beaufort

Margaret was a very clever woman. Her marriages were carefully chosen to give her the most power. She was constantly switching sides in the fight over the crown. She had proved that she was not loyal and that she would do whatever it took to get her son on the throne.

Margaret's **coat of arms**

Margaret's defence

I would never do anything to hurt the sons of my dear friend, Elizabeth. How could I possibly have agreed to a marriage between my son and Elizabeth's daughter if I'd had anything to do with her sons' disappearance? My **conscience** would not have allowed it.

Don't believe anything she says! She is a liar and will do anything for power!

Evidence: Henry VII

Before Henry married my daughter, Elizabeth of York, he had to tell everyone that my sons *did* have a true claim to the throne, despite Richard's rumours. If the princes did not have a claim, there was no point Henry marrying their sister to make his own claim stronger.

However, by admitting that their claim was true, he was creating a problem as they had a stronger claim to be king than him. He would have to get rid of my boys quickly so that he could still be king.

Elizabeth of York

Henry VII's defence

There had been no sight of the princes for two years before I arrived at the Tower of London. During that time, I was in **exile** in France. How could I possibly have had anything to do with it?

We all know that Richard III was responsible. He sent away most of the staff at the Tower so there were no witnesses.

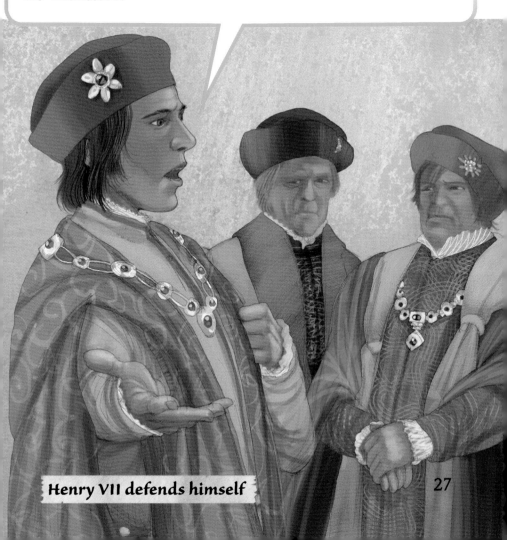

Henry VII defends himself

4 Suspect 3: Henry Stafford, Duke of Buckingham

Background

Like many people, the Duke of Buckingham was not loyal. Even though he was married to my sister, he was never loyal to my family.

Buckingham was with Richard III when they took Edward V to the Tower. He also helped to persuade people that the princes' claim to the throne was false and that Richard III was the true king.

Buckingham and Richard were very close. I know that Buckingham did some unpleasant (and illegal) things for Richard and probably kept a lot of his secrets.

Buckingham and Richard were very close.

Claim to the throne: strong

The Duke of Buckingham did have a claim to the throne. Three of his grandparents were descended from Edward III. In fact, he had a stronger claim than Henry VII. There is not much evidence to suggest that he wanted the throne for himself, though.

Henry Stafford,
Duke of Buckingham

Evidence

After Richard III was crowned king, he travelled around England. Richard left the Duke of Buckingham in London as **Constable** of the Tower – a position with a great deal of power.

When Richard returned, the two fell out. Perhaps Richard discovered what Buckingham had done to my sons.

It was clear that they did not sort out their quarrel, because Buckingham joined the plot with Margaret and me to remove Richard III from the throne.

Buckingham's defence

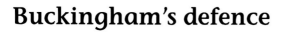

There's no evidence or **eyewitnesses** to say that I had anything to do with it. Richard and I did not fall out because he discovered what I had done. We fell out because *I* discovered what *he* had done.

If the princes were safe and well, why didn't he just show them in public to stop all the rumours?

5 What happened next?

In 1485, Henry VII launched another attack on Richard III. This was a great battle – one of the most important in England's history – the Battle of Bosworth Field.

Richard III was killed on the battlefield and Henry Tudor become King Henry VII.

The year after Henry became king, he married my daughter. Now I am in a position of power once more!

Timeline

9th April 1483:	30th April 1483:	1st May 1483:	16th June 1483:	22nd June 1483:	6th July 1483:
Edward IV dies	Richard takes Edward V to the Tower	Elizabeth takes her children to Westminster Abbey	Richard, Duke of York, joined Edward at the Tower of London	The princes' claim to the throne in doubt	Richard is crowned king

re-enactment of the Battle of Bosworth Field

When Henry VII became king, he did nothing to stop the rumours about my sons. He did not prove that they were alive and well, but he also did not say whether Richard had anything to do with their disappearance.

This caused Henry problems years later. A young man appeared, claiming to be my younger son, Richard of Shrewsbury.

Perkin Warbeck: the fake prince

Perkin Warbeck was born in Belgium and moved to Ireland when he was around 17 years old. This is where he learnt English.

He went to the Netherlands, where he spent time with my husband's sister, Margaret of York.

I do not know whether Margaret truly believed that Warbeck was my son (her nephew). However, she would have wanted revenge on Henry VII for killing her other brother, Richard III.

Perkin Warbeck

IRELAND

ENGLAND

NETHERLANDS

BELGIUM

On 3rd July 1495, Warbeck sailed to England. He wanted to defeat Henry VII and become king instead. However, he did not make it to shore and was quickly chased away by local soldiers.

Warbeck tried again in September 1497. He landed in Cornwall. Lots of people were unhappy about Henry VII's taxes there, so many joined Warbeck on the march to London.

But Warbeck was captured. He confessed that he was not the missing prince.

Surprisingly, Henry VII was kind to Warbeck. He was not even arrested, and was seen in the king's court.

However, the king was not so kind after Warbeck tried to escape. After that, Henry VII had Warbeck taken to the Tower of London.

Warbeck even planned an escape from there! His plan was discovered before he had a chance to try it though.

inside the Tower of London

6 Elizabeth Woodville summarises

When Henry VII came to the throne, it was the end of the fighting about which family would rule. It was the beginning of the Tudors!

Now, I finally have a high social position and power, and I am pleased that England is at peace. However, I still have unanswered questions about my sons …

The disappearance of my two princes is one of the greatest unsolved mysteries in history.

You have heard a lot of evidence about the three suspects. You have heard their motives and their defence. It is up to you to decide what you believe is true, to separate the facts from rumour, and to come to your own **conclusion** about who is responsible.

an 1878 painting of Edward V and Richard of Shrewsbury, Duke of York – the Princes in the Tower

Glossary

accusations suggestions that someone has done something bad

archery sport using a bow and arrow

coat of arms a picture to represent someone's family

conclusion a final decision

conscience part of your mind that tells you what is right or wrong

constable someone in a position to keep peace

crowned officially made a king or queen

descended from related to people in the past

exile sent away in punishment

eyewitnesses people who saw things with their own eyes

illegal not allowed by the law

motive reason to do something

re-enactment a show of something that has happened before

suspects people who might have done something

Tudor the time between 1485 and 1603 when the Tudor family ruled England

uprising an act against someone in power

Index

Discuss the arguments for and against each suspect

Henry VII and
Margaret Beaufort

Richard III

Henry Stafford,
Duke of Buckingham

Ideas for reading

Written by Christine Whitney
Primary Literacy Consultant

Reading objectives:
- be introduced to non-fiction books that are structured in different ways
- listen to, discuss and express views about non-fiction
- retrieve and record information from non-fiction
- discuss and clarify the meanings of words

Spoken language objectives:
- participate in discussion
- speculate, hypothesise, imagine and explore ideas through talk
- ask relevant questions

Curriculum links: History: Develop an awareness of the past; Writing: Write for different purposes

Word count: 2583

Interest words: accusations, conclusion, descended, suspects, motive

Resources: paper and pencils

Build a context for reading

- Ask the group to name any kings or queens they know of. Now show them a photograph of the Tower of London. Ask them for any facts they know about this place. Explain where the Tower of London is and that it may still be visited today.

- Before the children see the book, read the title to them *The Princes in the Tower: An Unsolved Mystery* and show them the cover image. Challenge children to make predictions about the content of the book.

- Introduce the words *accusations, conclusion, descended, suspects, motive*. Explain that these words will appear in the book. Ask children to work in pairs to suggest sentences which use two of these words correctly. Check understanding of correct usage and remind children to use the glossary when reading.

Understand and apply reading strategies

- Read together pages 2–13. Challenge children to summarise what happened to the two princes after their father's death and who are the three main suspects.